DOLPHINS

Please visit our web site at: www.garethstevens.com
For a free color catalog describing Gareth Stevens Publishing's
list of high-quality books and multimedia programs, call
1-800-542-2595 (USA) or 1-800-387-3178 (Canada).
Gareth Stevens Publishing's fax: (414) 332-3567.

Library of Congress Cataloging-in-Publication Data available upon
request from publisher. Fax (414) 336-0157 for the attention of the
Publishing Records Department.

ISBN 0-8368-4115-8

This edition first published in 2004 by '
Gareth Stevens Publishing
A World Almanac Education Group Company
330 West Olive Street, Suite 100
Milwaukee, Wisconsin 53212 USA

This U.S. edition copyright © 2004 by Gareth Stevens, Inc. Original edition
copyright © 2001 by DeAgostini UK Limited. First published in 2001 as
My Animal Kingdom: All About Dolphins by DeAgostini UK Ltd., Griffin House,
161 Hammersmith Road, London W6 8SD, England. Additional end matter
copyright © 2004 by Gareth Stevens, Inc.

Editorial and design: Tucker Slingsby Ltd., London
Gareth Stevens series editor: Catherine Gardner
Gareth Stevens art direction: Tammy Gruenewald

Picture Credits
NHPA — Andy Rouse: cover and title page; Gerard Lacz: 6-7, 17; Dr. Eckart Pott:
    9, 15, 17; Anthony Bannister: 12; Laurie Campbell: 16, 21; Rich Kirchner: 18-19;
    Norbert Wu: 20, 26; A.N.T.: 23; T. Kitchin and V. Hurst: 23; Henry Ausloos: 24-25;
    Patrick Fagot: 29.
Oxford Scientific Films — Konrad Wothe: 7, 19, 28, 29; Frank Schneidermeyer: 8;
    Tony Bomford and Tim Borrill: 10-11; John McCammon: 11; Howard Hall: 13, 24;
    Max Gibbs: 12; Daniel J. Cox: 14, 18; Clive Bromhall: 21; Richard Day: 22;
    Tony Bomford: 27; Doug Allan: 27; Jerry Cooke 28.

Printed in the United States of America

1 2 3 4 5 6 7 8 9 08 07 06 05 04

DOLPHINS

Gareth Stevens Publishing
A WORLD ALMANAC EDUCATION GROUP COMPANY

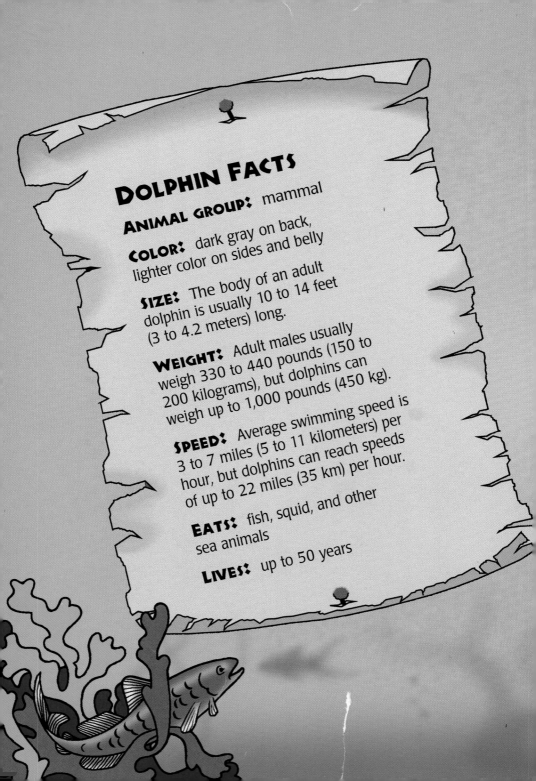

DOLPHIN FACTS

ANIMAL GROUP: mammal

COLOR: dark gray on back, lighter color on sides and belly

SIZE: The body of an adult dolphin is usually 10 to 14 feet (3 to 4.2 meters) long.

WEIGHT: Adult males usually weigh 330 to 440 pounds (150 to 200 kilograms), but dolphins can weigh up to 1,000 pounds (450 kg).

SPEED: Average swimming speed is 3 to 7 miles (5 to 11 kilometers) per hour, but dolphins can reach speeds of up to 22 miles (35 km) per hour.

EATS: fish, squid, and other sea animals

LIVES: up to 50 years

CONTENTS

Words that appear in the glossary
are printed in **boldface** type the
first time they occur in the text.

A Closer Look

Dolphins look like big fish, but they are not fish. They are **mammals**, like whales and people. Fish can breathe underwater, through their **gills**. Dolphins must swim to the surface of the water to breathe air through their **blowholes**. Fish swim by moving their tails from side to side. Dolphins swim by moving their large tail fins, called flukes, up and down. Dolphins are very good swimmers. Their flukes help them speed through the ocean, and they have flippers to help them steer, turn, and slow down.

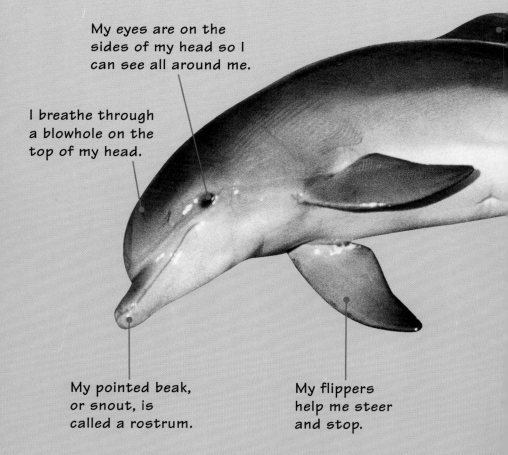

My eyes are on the sides of my head so I can see all around me.

I breathe through a blowhole on the top of my head.

My pointed beak, or snout, is called a rostrum.

My flippers help me steer and stop.

- When dolphins feed, they sometimes hit fish with their tails to stun them or to push them out of the water.

- Dolphins smack their tails on the water to send messages to each other.

- Balancing on their strong tails, dolphins can move backward across the surface of the water. They look like they are dancing on the water.

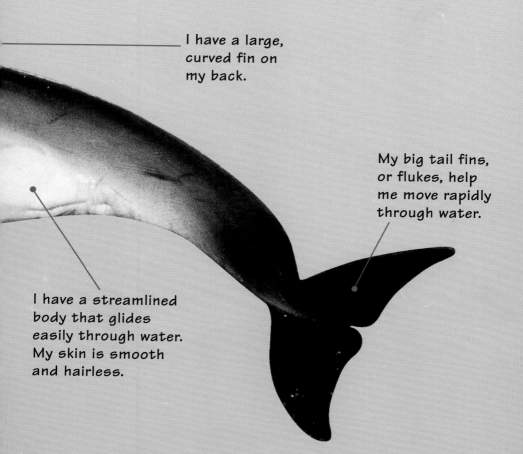

I have a large, curved fin on my back.

My big tail fins, or flukes, help me move rapidly through water.

I have a streamlined body that glides easily through water. My skin is smooth and hairless.

7

A dolphin has a big **brain**, which might be why dolphins have such good eyesight and hearing. A dolphin picks up sounds through its ears and lower jaws. It can hear sounds much lower and higher than the sounds people can hear. Dolphins use sounds to **communicate**.

One kind of dolphin, called a bottle-nosed dolphin, has a large, domed head with a short snout, or rostrum. About one hundred sharp, pointed teeth fit together like a zipper in its jaws. Its teeth help the dolphin grab and hold slippery fish and other **prey**.

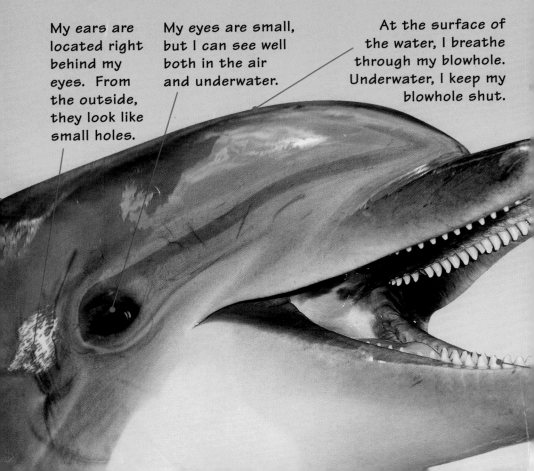

My ears are located right behind my eyes. From the outside, they look like small holes.

My eyes are small, but I can see well both in the air and underwater.

At the surface of the water, I breathe through my blowhole. Underwater, I keep my blowhole shut.

NOISY NOSES

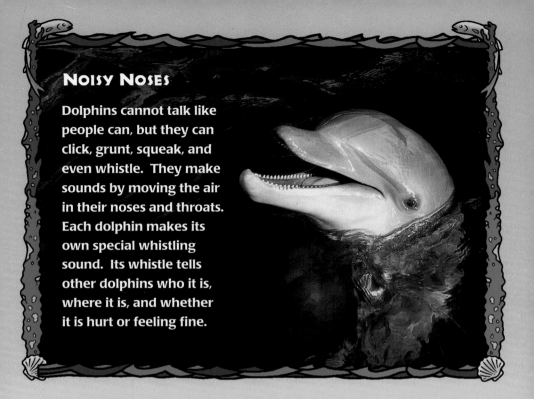

Dolphins cannot talk like people can, but they can click, grunt, squeak, and even whistle. They make sounds by moving the air in their noses and throats. Each dolphin makes its own special whistling sound. Its whistle tells other dolphins who it is, where it is, and whether it is hurt or feeling fine.

TOUGH TEETH

A bottle-nosed dolphin has lots of pointed teeth, but it cannot chew! It must swallow food whole and uses its teeth mainly to hold prey. As a dolphin grows, new layers are added to its teeth. People can tell the age of a dolphin by the number of layers on its teeth.

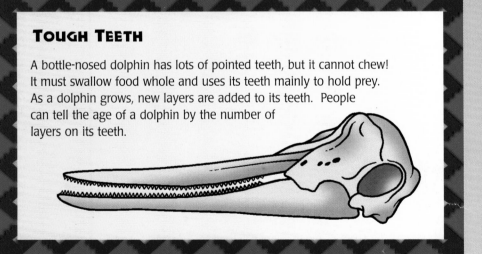

My sharp teeth are great for catching and holding fish.

Home, Sweet Home

The ocean is a great place for dolphins to live. It has lots of room for swimming and plenty of food. Bottle-nosed dolphins live in oceans all over the world, often staying in **bays** or **lagoons**. Some live in the open ocean — but not far from land.

Where in the World?

Ancestors of bottle-nosed dolphins swam in the oceans about five million years before people lived on Earth. Today, about thirty-two kinds of dolphins live in oceans, and in some rivers, in all parts of the world. Many kinds of dolphins stay in the same parts of the same oceans all year long. Dolphins that live in colder places, however, often travel to warmer waters in winter.

dolphin

porpoise

Dolphins and porpoises are related, and they look alike in many ways. The easiest way to tell them apart is by looking at the different shapes of their bodies and heads.

COOL COLORS

A dolphin can be hard to spot in the ocean. Seen from above, its dark back blends in with the dark color of deep water. Seen from below, its pale belly blends in with the ocean's bright surface. **Camouflage** helps dolphins hide from enemies as well as from the fish they need to catch for food.

NEIGHBORS

Dolphins share their ocean home with many other kinds of animals. Just above the water, seabirds dive into the waves to snatch passing fish. Tiny animals and plants, too small even to see, float in surface water, making a tasty soup that attracts hungry fish, whales, and other sea animals, including dolphins. At lower levels of the ocean, octopus, **squid**, fish, shellfish, jellyfish, and sea mammals swim in search of food and protection from the keen eyes of **predators**.

DEADLY HUNTERS

The ocean is full of predators hunting for a tasty meal. Some use poison to catch and kill their prey. The man-of-war jellyfish (*top left*) looks beautiful, but it is deadly. It floats on the surface of the water, with its long **tentacles** trailing below it. When a fish becomes tangled in the tentacles, it is quickly stung to death. An octopus (*bottom left*) hides on the ocean floor, waiting to pounce on passing prey. First, it uses its poisonous bite to stun the prey. Then, it grabs the prey with its eight tentacles. The suckers on the tentacles can hold on to even the slipperiest prey.

FANTASTIC FISH

Sea animals live everywhere, from shallow coastal waters to the deepest ocean floor, and include fish of all shapes and sizes. A giant manta ray, for example, can be 23 feet (7 meters) across and weigh as much as a car! With its big, black wings and horns, this huge fish looks scary, but it is harmless. It does not even have any teeth. The giant manta ray glides along the surface of the water, feeding on shrimps and small fish.

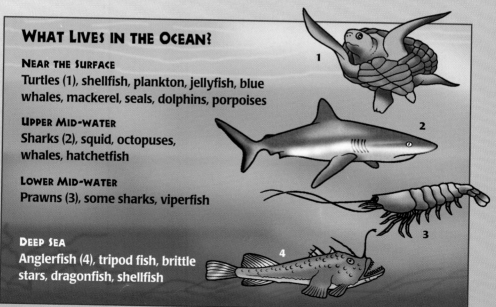

WHAT LIVES IN THE OCEAN?

NEAR THE SURFACE
Turtles (1), shellfish, plankton, jellyfish, blue whales, mackerel, seals, dolphins, porpoises

UPPER MID-WATER
Sharks (2), squid, octopuses, whales, hatchetfish

LOWER MID-WATER
Prawns (3), some sharks, viperfish

DEEP SEA
Anglerfish (4), tripod fish, brittle stars, dragonfish, shellfish

THE FAMILY

Bottle-nosed dolphins live in groups called pods. The size of a pod can be large or small. A pod of bottle-nosed dolphins usually has between two and fifteen members. In some parts of the world, however, a pod may include more than one hundred dolphins. Sometimes, several pods come together to form a school, or herd, that has hundreds of dolphins.

All of the members of a pod hunt prey and play together. If a dolphin is ill or injured, other dolphins in the pod push it to the surface of the water so it can breathe. All of the female dolphins in a pod help take care of the pod's young.

Depending on where a pod lives, baby dolphins, called calves, are born during either spring or summer. A female dolphin has one calf at a time, and the new mother takes good care of her calf. She whistles to it all the time to help it learn the sound of her call.

A calf stays close to its mother. Because it is not yet a very good swimmer, it relies on the movement of water made by its mother's swimming to help carry it along in the ocean. For food, a calf, at first, drinks only the milk its mother produces in her body, but the calf soon learns to eat fish and to hunt for itself.

Young dolphins stay with their mothers until they are about three years old. Then, female calves usually stay in the family pod, while most males leave to join other pods or to form new ones.

HELPING HAND

Dolphins must breathe air to live. When a newborn calf has trouble getting to the surface of the water for its first breath of air, the adult dolphins in the pod will give it a push.

BABY FILE

BIRTH

A bottle-nosed dolphin calf is born tail first. On the day it is born, the calf is already about one-third as long as its mother. A newborn calf is able to swim immediately after birth, and the first thing it must do is swim to the surface of the water for air. Dolphin calves feed on the rich milk produced in their mothers' bodies, but all of the dolphins in a pod help take care of the calves. Within a few days after it is born, a calf learns to make noises and talk to other dolphins.

THREE TO SIX MONTHS

When it is a few months old, a dolphin calf starts to get its teeth and can eat fish, but it still drinks its mother's milk, too. A very young calf stays close to its mother. As it gets older, the calf will wander farther from its mother to dive and play with other dolphins.

EIGHTEEN MONTHS TO THREE YEARS

A dolphin calf usually begins to eat solid food when it is six months old, but it may also feed on its mother's milk until it is about eighteen months old. A calf stays with its mother for about three years, but even after it can take care of itself, a young dolphin will stay with its family pod for a long time. A female dolphin may stay with her family pod her whole life.

LIFE AT SEA

A dolphin's body is designed for swimming. It has smooth, hairless skin that glides easily through the ocean. Under its skin, it has a layer of fat, called blubber, that helps it float and keeps it warm. Its streamlined shape allows it to speed through the water and to dive and leap above the surface. Paddlelike flippers and powerful tail fins, called flukes, make dolphins strong and graceful swimmers.

DID YOU KNOW?

An animal that lives in water can grow bigger than an animal that lives on land because the water will help support its heavy body. The blue whale is the biggest animal in the world. It is more than 98 feet (30 m) long and almost twenty-five times as heavy as an elephant, which is the heaviest animal that lives on land.

HOLD IT!

Dolphins need air to breathe, just as people do. A dolphin swims to the surface of the water, opens its blowhole, and blows out the air in its lungs. Then, it gulps in fresh air, closes its blowhole, and dives into the waves. Underwater, a dolphin holds its breath. An adult dolphin can stay underwater for up to fifteen minutes and can dive as deep as 650 feet (200 m).

LONG JUMPERS

Bottle-nosed dolphins are fast swimmers. They can reach speeds of almost 25 miles (40 kilometers) per hour for short periods of time. They travel fastest by leaping out of the water in a series of long jumps.

FAVORITE FOODS

Bottle-nosed dolphins must hunt for their food. They eat many different kinds of fish, as well as shellfish and squid. Adult dolphins can eat more than 40 pounds (18 kilograms) of fish a day. They spend about eight hours a day looking for food and eating it. A bottle-nosed dolphin will hunt for its food either alone or in organized groups. In a group hunt, the dolphins form a circle around a large **shoal** of fish and herd the fish together. Then the dolphins take turns swimming through the mass of fish to feed.

EATING HABITS
Bottle-nosed dolphins swallow fish headfirst so that rough scales or sharp spines do not get caught in their throats. They tear larger fish into smaller pieces by shaking them or by rubbing them on the ocean floor.

SPLASH!

Dolphins love to leap high out of the water and land with a big splash. They also like to swim on their backs and slap the water with their fins. Sometimes, dolphins leap, do tricks, and splash just for fun. At other times, their splashing is a way to hunt prey. Fish scared by a dolphin's splashing will swim into a tight bunch. Then the dolphin can easily swallow mouthfuls of them.

LEFTOVERS

Dolphins often follow fishing boats. They have learned to catch fish attracted to fishing bait and to grab any small fish that are tossed overboard.

DID YOU KNOW?

Hunting dolphins use sound to find food. A bottle-nosed dolphin can make as many as one thousand click sounds a second. When these sounds reach objects in the water, such as shoals of fish, they bounce off, creating an **echo**. Hearing the echoes, a dolphin can tell how big the fish are and where they are located. Finding objects with sound is known as echolocation.

Danger!

Dolphins are ocean predators, but they are also prey for other ocean predators. Although dolphins do not have many enemies, hungry sharks and killer whales will hunt and kill young bottle-nosed dolphins. In a group, the dolphins can defend themselves. Sometimes, they will even gang up to attack a shark! Besides watching out for ocean predators, dolphins must also beware of people. Each year, thousands of dolphins die in fishing nets.

Nasty Nets

When dolphins become tangled in fishing nets, they cannot swim to the surface to breathe, and they drown. In the past thirty years, more than seven million dolphins have died this way.

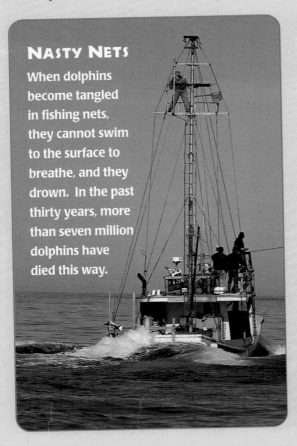

Terrible Teeth

A tiger shark (*right*) may be the most ferocious hunter of all the ocean predators. It can sniff out prey over a wide area. Just one drop of blood in millions of drops of water is often enough to catch the attention of a hungry tiger shark. Its razor-sharp teeth can slice through flesh and bone with one bite, and it will eat almost anything it catches, including a dolphin. A small, young dolphin swimming alone is an especially easy catch for a tiger shark.

FRIEND OR FOE?

The large killer whale, or orca, belongs to the same group of animals as the dolphin — but the two are not friends. Orca work as a team to find prey. They drive the prey to the shore, where it cannot escape, then they attack. Their sharp teeth can easily tear huge chunks of meat out of their cornered prey.

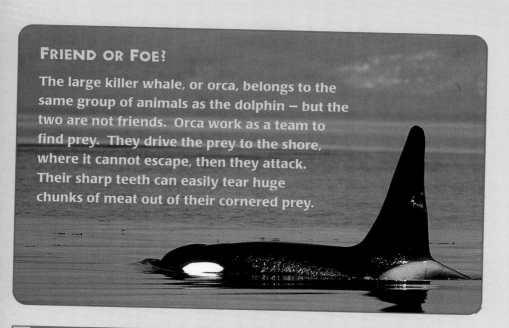

A Dolphin's Day

5:00 AM

I heard fishing boats in the bay. I went to see if I could find any fish scraps to eat.

6:00 AM

I didn't have much luck with the boats, but my pod joined another pod, and we went fishing together. We heard a huge shoal of fish outside the bay.

9:00 AM

Joining the other pod made for great hunting, and we had a good, fishy feast. After eating, I felt nice and full — and sleepy — so I dozed for a while.

12:00 NOON

After a good sleep, it was time to play! The Sun was shining, and it sparkled on the water as I leaped and twisted through the waves. I joined some other dolphins in a game of tag, and we danced backward over the waves on our tails.

1:00 PM

It was time to rest again! I lazed in the waves as some of the young dolphins played tug-of-war with seaweed. I thought about all the skills I had learned as a young dolphin from playing games.

2:00 PM A boat full of humans came to watch us, so we leaped, rolled, splashed, and chattered at them. We put on quite a show. A few humans swam in the water with us.

 3:00 PM I was feeling hungry, so I went on a little fishing trip.

 4:00 PM Near the ocean floor, I came across a group of squid. They made a very tasty snack!

 6:00 PM After another good snooze, I was ready for some serious hunting. The pod we met earlier joined my pod again. Teamwork makes for better hunting and eating.

 7:00 PM We herded a big shoal of fish into shallow water, so we all had plenty to eat.

 9:00 PM As the Sun began to set, we swam out farther in the ocean, leaping through the waves. I could leap higher than any other dolphin in the pod.

 12:00 MIDNIGHT I was on lookout. The females and the young dolphins were sleeping at the surface of the water. I swam around to make sure no sharks or killer whales were lurking nearby.

 2:00 AM At last, it was my turn to sleep. Other dolphins in the pod took their turns keeping watch. The young calves stayed close to their mothers for safety.

 5:00 AM It will be dawn soon and time to hunt for another tasty breakfast.

RELATIVES

Dolphins, whales, and porpoises are all related. They belong to a large group of animals that live in water their whole lives. The animals in this group have much in common. They all have blowholes, paddle-shaped front flippers, and a thick layer of blubber under their skin. They do not have hair, claws, back legs, or ears that stick out from their bodies. Some members of this group, such as blue whales and humpback whales, do not have any teeth. They are called **baleen** whales. The rest of the group, including dolphins and porpoises, do have teeth.

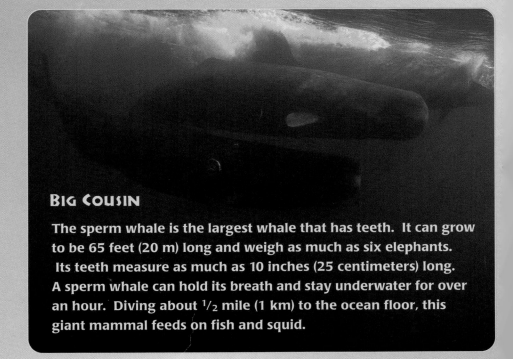

BIG COUSIN

The sperm whale is the largest whale that has teeth. It can grow to be 65 feet (20 m) long and weigh as much as six elephants. Its teeth measure as much as 10 inches (25 centimeters) long. A sperm whale can hold its breath and stay underwater for over an hour. Diving about ¹/₂ mile (1 km) to the ocean floor, this giant mammal feeds on fish and squid.

PLATES FOR FOOD

The right whale is a baleen whale.
Instead of having teeth in its mouth, it
has bony, fringelike plates called baleen.
The baleen helps the whale eat by filtering
food out of the seawater. To feed, the whale
swims slowly across the ocean's surface, holding
its huge jaws wide open to take in big gulps of water.
Tiny creatures in the water get caught on the baleen. The
whale scrapes them off with its tongue and swallows them.

SMALL COUSIN

Like dolphins, porpoises
have blowholes, flippers,
blubber, and teeth, but they
are smaller than dolphins
and do not have beaks. A
type of porpoise called the
common porpoise feeds on
fish, either swallowing them
whole or chopping them up
with its spade-shaped teeth.

HUMANS AND DOLPHINS

Dolphins have charmed people for thousands of years, and many folktales tell about dolphins that saved sailors from drowning. Bottle-nosed dolphins are probably the best-known dolphins in the world because they are the type of dolphins that usually perform tricks in shows at zoos and **marine parks**. In the 1960s, a bottle-nosed dolphin named Flipper was the star of a very popular television series.

WILD THINGS

Bottle-nosed dolphins are easy to train, and they are popular performers in shows at many zoos and marine parks. The crowds love to watch dolphins leap through hoops, juggle balls, and eat fish out of a trainer's hands. At some parks, visitors can feed and pat dolphins. Many people, however, believe that keeping dolphins in **captivity** and making them do tricks is wrong. They think all dolphins should live in the wild.

CAUTION!

Dolphins that live close to the shore often get used to being around humans. Some dolphins even let people swim with them, and some people travel a long way for a chance to swim with the dolphins. Swimming with dolphins, however, can be very dangerous. A predator cannot tell the difference between a dolphin and a person.

Dolphins help each other. They protect any sick or injured dolphins from predators, nudge newborns to the water's surface for air, and have even been known to push drowning humans to safety.

STAR TURN

For thousands of years, people have painted and made carvings of dolphins. Ancient Greeks and

Delphinus

Romans considered dolphins sacred. A dolphin even appears in the sky as a constellation, which is a pattern of stars that forms the shape of an object.

GLOSSARY

BALEEN
Bony plates that hang like fringe from the upper jaw of a whale that does not have teeth. The comblike fringes strain tiny plants and animals out of the seawater so the whale can eat them.

BAYS
Small bodies of water that extend into the land around a main ocean or lake.

BLOWHOLES
Small openings on the heads of whales and dolphins, which open to the animals' nostrils and are used for breathing.

BRAIN
An organ inside the skull that controls thought and movement.

CAMOUFLAGE
A color, pattern, or appearance that helps an animal blend in with its surroundings.

CAPTIVITY
The condition of being kept in a place without a chance to leave.

COMMUNICATE
To exchange information by using particular sounds, symbols, or behaviors.

ECHO
A sound that has bounced off of an object and back into the air.

GILLS
The organs fish use to breathe underwater.

LAGOONS
Shallow ponds located near, or connected to, larger bodies of water.

MAMMALS
Warm-blooded animals that have backbones and hair or fur on their skin and that feed their young with milk from the mothers' bodies.

MARINE PARKS
Outdoor areas designed to keep sea animals in a safe environment where people can come to see them and learn about them.

PREDATORS
Animals that kill other animals for food.

PREY
Animals that a predator hunts and kills for food.

SHOAL
A large group.

SQUID
A sea animal, related to the octopus, that has a long, tapered body with eight short and two usually longer armlike tentacles.

TENTACLES
The long flexible "arms" of an animal such as a jellyfish, a squid, or an octopus.

INDEX